The Shofar of Poetry

God Inspired Poetry & Words of Encouragement to Break the Chains of Bondage

©T.T.Taylor

This is dedicated to the one and only Savior of my soul…
God
These are His words…A testimony to His power and
greatness.

I love you

Table of Context

Foreword

I have had the privilege and honor of writing a foreword for a book that, I believe, is needed not only for ministry, but, for the world to recuperate from being spiritually bound by oppression. The Shofar of Poetry simply does a miraculous job with bringing you to a sense of peace. My big sister in ministry is a writer who is very instrumental in writing, teaching and preaching in the prophetic. Tamara executes all three of those things throughout the course of this book and has you ready to praise God by sounding the shofar.

For those that don't know, a shofar is a musical instrument that is made from the horn of a ram for religious purposes. One of the uses of the shofar that I love is in the book of Joshua when Joshua and his troops go into Jericho. On the seventh day upon walking around Jericho seven times, when given the signal, they shouted and blew the shofar and the walls came crashing down. Do you want to feel the glory of God? Are you ready to receive this blessing from the Most High upon reading this book? You are truly in for a treat. This book of prophetic anointing will minister to your life and your spirit will be at rest. This book is needed for a generation of people who constantly wonder if God is there. This book is needed to shake the foundations of those who might be bound by confusion, depression, oppression and will be free from every trial and tribulation. This book is needed for all of humanity and I speak a blessing that upon your completion of this book, your mind and your life will be changed and you will no longer be confused nor worried about anything. Get ready to sound the shofar!

-Reverend Lee R. E. Brown III "Tre"
<u>Grace CME Church, New Britain CT</u>

The Shofar of Poetry
God Inspired Poetry & Words of Encouragement to Break the Chains of Bondage

The Yearning for God's Presence

Burden of Love

Laying here just basking
His Glory weighs upon me
Like that of a warm body
His expression of love to me

Tears streaming down my face
Worship flows through my very being
His burden of love for me
A continual though weighing heavily

The burden of persecution
The carrying of the cross
The nailing of hands and feet
Is so unbearable, the complex thought

No human being
Has a love so great
To suffer for a sinful people
He was charged with such a weight

And now I
A sinful creature
Made new by His love and grace
Beholds and esteems His glory
Longing to seek His face

Needing Him to see me
Wanting Him to consume me

Asking Him to reside in me
Waiting for His response to me

Eagerly awaiting
Passionately seeking
My intimate time with Him
Which in past times were fleeting

Now I know
And refuse to go without
The weight of His glory
From His burden of love, there is no doubt

That

His love surpasses
The beautiful blue skies
The length of the calm seas
The majesty of high peaks and mountains
Even the love people would have for me

Jesus' burden of love
Was something he held an honor
To do what His Father told him to do
He will always remain that Man of valor

Untitled (God Speaks)

I hear a soft voice
Whispering sweetly in my ear
Saying,
"Do not to be afraid
For I just want you near..."
Nearer my God to thee?
"I want you to draw from me
So I can show you
The very things I see
Just open up your heart to receive
My spirit
My love
My anointing from above
My peace
My joy
Come on!
No need to be coy...
I just want to give you
Just a bit of myself
To equip you
Shield you
And guard you
When times get a bit rough...
Don't just keep it
All to yourself
For they will overcome
By the word of your testimony
So let this mind be in you
To share what is rich
And holds so much wealth!

I have given you dreams
Placed in your sight visions
I've placed the hot coal on your lips
To speak with authority
My word into all nations
My child
I have appointed you
For this time and place
I have heard your prayers
You long to see My face,
But to see My face
You must kill your flesh
No man has seen me and lived
Your earthly self must be crushed!
I love you, daughter
Even when you fell
I stayed my hand upon you
So you can live and tell,
Of all the things
I have delivered you from
But now is the time
And this time you must not run...
There is no need to fear
For that is not of Me,
I will give you what to say
When to say and how your tone must be...
No matter what people say
Do not ever have a doubt
I have called you from your mother's womb
I will surely break you out!
Your gifts are making room for you
You feel me in you gut
Even in those dark times

When you feel you're in a rut...
But, my love
You've never ceased to amaze me
No matter the test or trial
You always manage to rise up
When others have left you to die!
So continue to listen
To my voice in your ear
I will never leave nor forsake you
I, my child, will always be near

Do You Have Power?

*But you will receive power when the Holy Spirit comes upon you.
And you will be my witnesses, telling people about me everywhere
– in Jerusalem, throughout Judea, in Samaria, and to the ends of
the earth (Acts 1:8 NLT)*

On the day of Pentecost all the believers were meeting together
in one place. Suddenly, there was a sound from heaven like the
roaring of a mighty windstorm, and it filled the house where
they were sitting. Then, what looked like flames or tongues of
fire appeared and settled on each of them. And everyone
present was filled with the Holy Spirit and began speaking in
other languages, as the Holy Spirit gave them this ability (Acts
2:1 - 2:4 NLT)

Then Peter stepped forward with the eleven other apostles and
shouted to the crowd, "Listen carefully, all of you, fellow Jews
and residents of Jerusalem! Make no mistake about this. These
people are not drunk, as some of you are assuming. Nine o'clock
in the morning is much too early for that. No, what you see was
predicted long ago by the prophet Joel:

*'In the last days,' God says,
'I will pour out my Spirit upon all people.
Your sons and daughters will prophesy.
Your young men will see visions,
and your old men will dream dreams In those days I will pour out
my Spirit
even on my servants – men and women alike –
and they will prophesy.*

And I will cause wonders in the heavens above
and signs on the earth below **(Acts 2:14-2:19a NLT)**

Sitting here thinking about a conversation (via a social media messenger tool) when I began to speak some pretty intimate thoughts on the power of prayer and power of the Holy Spirit. My friend sent me a video clip of a woman of God who spoke about the power of prayer at a time in her life when everything was crashing down around her all at once! Aside from her father, both of her grandfathers, her Grandmother, I believe, and her were hit with pretty big diagnoses that could ultimately change their lives forever! She told her doctor to give her ONE WEEK! She prayed and petitioned God, with the power of the Holy Ghost and because she did that WITH HER BELIEVING AND NEVER DOUBTING, she was able to see God do the SUPERNATURAL! Healing took place in not only her life but in the lives the others she prayed for!

I said that to say this.... Today's churches are professing that this is the year of SUPERNATURAL something, whether it be blessings, success, miracles, whatever, but what I have come to realize that unless you believe with EVERYTHING YOU'VE GOT, unless YOU REALLY HAVE RECEIVED THE HOLY GHOST, no matter how much you profess it, it will not occur...

The scriptures tell us that WHEN you receive the Holy Spirit, you WILL receive POWER! Your words will have power, your prayers will carry power, you will be able to speak to the mountains in your life and tell it to move and it will do just that!!! But you have to be filled with the Holy Spirit!!!

The power of the Holy Spirit is vital to the church today because prophecy of the Word has to be fulfilled before Christ returns! So, for those who are on the fence about certain things like Prophets, healing hands, delivering prayers and so on, you may need to check with the Lord, in prayer, to ask Him to reveal to you if you have even received the Holy Ghost!! Not trying to be funny at all! I know sometimes we all have our brief moments of doubt. Thomas even doubted when Jesus came back after His crucifixion. Until Jesus told him to put his finger where they nailed him to the cross and in his side where they pierced him he didn't believe Jesus revealed himself to the disciples until then, which about one week later.

We need Holy Ghost power of we are to do ANYTHING today! We need it especially since we have been proclaiming Supernatural things in the body of Christ! The Holy Spirit is needed for such a time as this!

The Struggle

<u>Broken (Tug of War)</u>

Which way am I going?
Which way should I turn?
My heart and my mind are at a tug of war,
My heart yearns, but the flesh burns...

Broken in so many ways
I can't begin to tell you why
'Cause my heart wants to follow You
But my flesh is pulling... Just balled up in a corner to

Cry

Because

This flesh wants what it wants
My heart does too
My flesh wants to do wrong
But my heart
My soul
My spirit wants You!!

So broken inside I fall to my knees
Pleading
Praying
Asking You for some kind of relief

My tears are heavy
They come too many to count

Creating a pool, filling way over my head
Wanting to get this flesh completely out

Of

The will of the world
Wanting to die so You can live
Live within me so you can shine
Through me
Through my voice
Bring me out of hiding!!

But this flesh!!!

Keeps me at a tug of war!
Wanting what it wants
Breaking me into pieces
Breaking my heart of hearts...

I need a complete
Mental
Emotional
Spiritual
Make over

The ultimate overhaul

The main tug in this war
That will overthrown my flesh
The biggest breaking point of my life
The shift that will break the flesh of my flesh!

None of my bone will be saturated
With nothing but You, Lord
Your love, spirit will be all throughout me
Then I will draw others to come aboard!

The conviction of my sins
Drew me closer to thee
Now my flesh is dead
Now, You reign in me...

The tug of war is no longer
I will rise and I will set with You
To praise and worship You is what I live for
To speak for You is what I will do!!

My broken flesh allowed me
To here You in the midst
In the midst of all the hell I was going through
I thank God I finally got the gist!!

Being broken is more than a process
It is a place to see what needs to die
It is a place when God meets you and heals
He mends
He heals
Now you can rely

On

The miraculous powers of the one and only
The true and living God
Now I shall live and shall not die

No more tug of war
But walking
Hand in hand
With my God

Who cannot
And will not
Lie...

<u>My Heart</u>

My heart is a place
Where
Only God should dwell,

But
From the moment I saw you
It began to swell

The thoughts
The visions
The need to have you

Superseded
The thoughts and visions of God
He gave me only to view

Not knowing you had
A hidden agenda
For me

To lose sight
Of all
That was good

You used me
Shamed me
To receive my all

But to receive from you
Would not be possible
Even if you could

A picture
Is not worth
1000 words

And seeing
Is nowhere near
Believing

But looks and charm
Can be
Misinterpreted

And
You have made
Seeing very deceiving

Behind shifty eyes
You still wore
A mask

To speak with you
Would go in
One direction

I thought it was about us
It became clear
It was all about you

Your selfish thoughts
Would produce
Such a task

Sometimes
In order to win
You have to lose

Lose the thing
That has brought
You much grief

My need to win
Is needed more
Than a warm body

So

I chose to lose
Him
And all of my unbelief

He didn't keep me
When
I needed to be kept

He didn't hold me
Whenever
I sobbed and wept

Support
Was nowhere for me

In his vocabulary

But I made him
Look very good
To be there when need be

Now
I'm back in love
With my only true love

Where
My hands fit in His
Snug as a glove

Throughout my ordeal
When I was out
Of His realm

He still
Beckoned to me
When I didn't want to

Overwhelm

Him of my issues
That I created
All by myself

Knowing that He still loves me
Has given me
So much wealth

He whispers
To me
Speaking positive things

Giving me counsel
When I need it
Wrapping me in His wings

He told me
He would, He could
Never forget me

For I am
On His mind
All the time

While I was away
He wrote my name
In the palms of His hands

For
He knew I would be back
With Him some day,

To stand...

Believing in His word
Living it out
Day by day,

Resting in His arms
Just listening to Him

Telling me what to say...

Giving in to Him
At all costs
In every breath,

Taking Him, more into my heart
Absorbing Him
Until my last breath....

The Cost of the Anointing

I didn't know who you were
The day I heard you calling
Into a pit of despair
This particular day, I was falling...
But I read in your word
How you called Your chosen by voice
My heart was so elated
I couldn't have made a better choice...
But!
To answer your very call
And to render out a YES!
But I didn't know how my life would change,
To the point where I second guessed...
I began to pray and ask you
Where did my anointing lie?
My spirit began to burn with your word
All I can remember was saying, "Why?"
First you gave me a dream,
This was in very clear view
You even showed me what shoes I wore
You showed me what I was to do!
With a colorful robe, you adorned me
But I'm thinking
"My mind is playing tricks on me!"
Why would you want to use someone like me?
To stand in front of your people, seriously? Me?
Not doing the typical thing
Not running, well, not exactly,
I still did my thing
But, I never got caught acting...

Out of sorts...
Because I was starting to see the light
Pleading with you wanting to live right
But now I'm losing friends left and right
Because I'm not having fun, no delight
In
Going to the club
Getting my rum and coke
The occasional morale boosting
Getting my ego stroked...
I felt so bad
I felt so filthy
I separated from you
Not knowing you would still be with me!
Then seven years
And two kids later
A tugging at my heart
My spirit quietly hearing...
Your voice
In the still, empty space
Where you've always were
Now I hear the man of God!
My past became a blur!
Because You
Spoke to a place
I thought had died!
You
Gave me freedom
I once thought I denied!
Your love,
Lifted me in ways
I could never comprehend
My sins

You bared them
When I raised my hands
Surrendered my flesh
Gave you my heart
And with deep cry
YES!
Your Holy Spirit reigned
On me that one Sunday
Because the cost of Your Anointing
Paved the road you laid,
Though
I turned it into
Such a crooked and messy line
You straightened it all up
But, I don't dare think all is fine...
For the enemy will try
To come back at me
To claim a soul
That was never promised for him to keep...
But now!
I know what weapons to use
To square with him, toe to toe
Because the cost of my anointing
I choose not to forgo!

I Am Gomer (The Irony Of Completion)

This man has taken me to be his wife
Sincerely, I don't know why,
He is not what or who I long for
So, I'm struggling just being in his life!

I've slept with one man
Turned and slept with another
Then, ultimately, slept with my husband
Now, I have become a mother

Jezreel was my first born son
He was called so by The Lord
His name "God Scatters"
For His people will be cast away and cold...

Then, I brought forth a daughter
There's no telling her father is, as well,
For my adulteress ways there is no peace
I can only pray she lives well...

Lo-Ruhamah, I was told to name her
God will have no mercy, is what she means,
Because my sins are like the sins of this nation
But, right now, there's no means to to get clean...

Lo-Ammi is the name of my son
My third child after my daughter's weaning,
He said "We are not His people, He's not our God"
Oh Lord, my flesh is feening!!!

Now, I'm out in the cold
No food no shelter for me

I will go find a lover to take care of me
Since my husband has caused me to flee...

I can find no lover
To pay me what I need
I can't find not one friend
No one to sow a seed

I'm so far out there
Leaving my children and husband alone
Because my flesh was so needy
I am beyond far gone

Alone in the wilderness
I hear a sweet, sweet voice
Lulling me to come hither
For I had to make a choice

My husband has come to restore me
An adulterer , but, with a brand new start
To be forgiven of my transgressions
To love my husband with all my heart

For my husband came to reclaim me
Purchasing me at a common slave's rate
For his love for me ran very deep
Although I was one he did not date...

For the love of my husband was so deep
I realized God's love runs deeper
For He sent for me through the love of my husband
I guess, I am worthy... I am a keeper...

No More Flipping Tables

Then Jesus went into the temple of God and drove out all those who bought and sold in the temple, and overturned the tables of the money changers and the seats of those who sold doves And He said to them, "It is written, 'My house shall be called a house of prayer, 'but you have made it a 'den of thieves.' "(Matthew 21:12-13 NKJV)

I have to admit, my spirit was very grieved on this past Sunday during worship service. I was thinking about what the Lord showed me and all that He has spoken to me and the Glory coming in to take residence, burning up all things that are false and that are untrue in the house of God! He spoke to me and told me He was going to make the crooked places straight and how He was going to do everything to make God's church great! He has shown us a glimpse of what He wants to do in His house but it's just been that....
Now, please, don't get me wrong, I believe EVERYTHING He has spoken to me and I believe He will do just what He said, but, in order for Him to do what He said, we have to do our part...

Our part is to SEEK GOD! Fast, pray, study His word and hide it in our hearts, examine ourselves DAILY, most importantly, we must sit still and listen to Him when He speaks!

I was kind of shaken up when the Lord put this word in my spirit because I was trying to figure out what ties these scriptures to what He has placed in my spirit... As I was seeking Him and praying, He showed me this in an open vision: I saw Jesus walking into the sanctuary; He sees service going on as usual... choir singing, people dancing, shouting, clapping their hands and worshipping Him. There was a smile upon Jesus' face as if He was pleased! Then, everything came to an abrupt halt! The singing, dancing, praising and worshipping stopped! Tradition stepped in and quenched, grieved the Holy Spirit and Jesus' face frowned and was looking like it was in unbearable pain! So much so, he appeared in the front of the church and destroyed the altar area!

Forgive me if it seems as if I'm re-writing the scripture, GOD KNOWS I AM NOT!! But this is what was placed in my spirit during service and more so after service was over... It was about the anger of the Lord!

He is sick and tired of being robbed out of His praise, out of His worship! He is not a God of TRADITION, but He is a God that can do what He wants, how He wants, through whom He wants!! He is not a God that honors programs and timeframe! But He is a God that is jealous and who is WORTHY of all the praise and worship! When we are in His presence, we should not be consumed with whose around us, what they're doing and how they react to us when we give God our all!! But we should be UNDIGNIFIED!! Our worship should be no holds barred, unlimited!!!

When we limit our praise, our worship, out adoration towards The Father, it grieves Him! It grieves Him so much He flips over tables because He is not pleased! He is angry because His children would rather follow tradition than allow the spirit of God to move and take COMPLETE CONTROL! Not just in worship but in our daily lives!!

Think about it.... In the scripture, He turned over the tables in the temple because there were people buying and selling things...IN THE TEMPLE!!! He drove them out because they were disrespecting the House of God! Anyone who loves God and loves God's house know better than to do anything of the sort! God's house IS a house of prayer! God's house is HOLY GROUND!!! Not a den of thieves!!!

When we don't let the Holy Spirit flow, we are robbing God!!! So, He has every right to be angry! And because He is, He is saying that *UNTIL WE DO RIGHT BY HIM, HE WILL NOT DWELL AMONG US!! He says WHEN I SEND A WORD TO YOU; I SEND IT SO YOU CAN DO JUST WHAT I HAVE COMMANDED YOU TO DO! CORRECTION HAS TO COME TO MY HOUSE BEFORE I TAKE RESIDENCE!! MY GLORY WILL NOT FALL UPON YOU UNTIL YOU CLEAN UP ALL THAT HAS BEEN INSTRUCTED FOR YOU TO CLEAN UP, says The Lord!*

When God spoke to Moses by way of the burning bush, he told him to remove his shoes because he was standing on Holy Ground! We have lost respect for the House of God! We have placed people in position that has not been called for said position, desecrating not just the position held, but, the body of Christ as a whole!!

We have to come to the understanding that God is coming back for His bride!! But she has to be WITHOUT SPOT OR WRINKLE!!! Do we want Jesus to continue flipping over the tables? Do we want to anger Him over and over again?? Do we want to disrespect Him? He gave His life for us!! Why would we not do what He is asking us to do!! He is speaking to God on our behalf and to continue to do the things we are doing and not checking ourselves daily, we will not be with Him when He returns for us!!!

NO MORE FLIPPING TABLES!!!

The Presence of God

Prophetic Poems of Encouragement

Beyond The Veil

Far
Beyond my own imagination
Was a vision The Lord gave me
With no mistake in its interpretation

The people of God
In the house of God
Glorifying
Admiring
Loving on God

Some standing in awe
Some with tears in their eyes
Some were body bowed and knee bent
Some on the floor their bodies lie

With no instruments wailing a tune
No choir singing in harmony
But the sweet melodic sounds of true worshippers
Crying out, awaiting God's glory

In my spirit I feel a pulling
An urge, a yearning to seek Him
As the voices of the saints get louder
My language changes, calling on Elohim!

Our cries were not such of sorrow
They were not cries of defeat
Our cries were not anything mournful
But our cries reached Christ's ear, tweaked

In the spirit, I felt the earth quake
Looking up, the very ceiling was cracked
God's glory fell upon us as the very veil
Ripped from top to bottom, front and back

The people of God worshipped
Slain in the spirit
Not an eye was dry or open in the room
As the Glory of God remained in it

The veil covered the entire sanctuary
Looking at the rip the Lord spoke to me
"Daughter, this is the veil from the temple
The rip means you now have access to Me

Although, it will be difficult
For no one has seen Me and lived
It doesn't mean you will surely die
But your flesh must submit and you must be cleaned

The blood of the Lamb
The sacrifice of yourself
The genuine love for Me
Has got to die, to be engulfed

With My Glory
With My shine
With My radiance
By spending time

With Me

Your God
Your Savior
Your Rod

Your all and all
Your Alpha and Omega
Your salvation
Your Rose of Sharon!

The weight of His Glory
Surpassed my feeble comprehension
Applying pressure, the spiritual surgery
No anesthesia, but spiritual sedation

Allowing God to endow me
With His anointing, His precious spirit
Released the burden that weighed me down
Freeing me to worship Him deliberately...

He
Manifested Himself
In a room full of His people
All of whom were drawn
To seek Him freely!

His Hem (Prophetic Demonstration)

Intense pain
Excruciating beyond belief
suffering in silence
Praying for some relief...

Though I was praying
Night after night I bowed
I thought He didn't hear a word
As if I was lost in a crowd...

Searching for medical answers
To find a sure fire remedy
My doctors couldn't find any
Not one, two or three...

Singing a sad tune
For I'm not sure what's to be
Trying to lift my spirits
All I keep thinking is bleed

Blood flow bleeding
Issue
Issue of blood
Woman in the bible needing

A miracle
A healing
A solution of desperation
Not wasting time, is fleeting!!

Placing myself
In herself
In my private prayer time
Physically reaching for

MY HELP!
My help comes from Him!
Prophetic demonstration
I reach for the hem

Of

His garment
So that I can be made whole
whatsoever is a bold
Notion
To reach up into thin air

And

Claim my healing
From a God
Who is the Master
Of all things

So...

With comfort in knowing this...

I sleep

Only to awaken the next day

Going about my daily regimen
Just to begin praising Him

Because I prophetically
Touched His Hem
Demonstrating my belief

In His word
Never giving any clout
To anything within my mind
Even when glimpses of doubt

Tried

To rear its ugly head
Making me think
I was a step closer to dead
But...

Putting action to work
Shows the Lord will work
And turn His works
Into

Miracles!!

Prayer Shawl

Under the shadow
Of the Almighty
Draping my prayer shawl
Over my head like a hoodie...

Covering myself
In His Love
In His Protection
In His presence from above,

Meditation of the heart
Gut wrenching desire from the soul
Elevated pulsing in my spirit
Are words, never shared, never told...

As my eyes are closed
I see only what He would allows
My prayer language gets much deeper
His presence falls on me like a cloud,

I am wrapped up in His glory
He allows me to see His face
He tells me to not be afraid
For He has given me grace...

My flesh was sacrificed
As I
Bow before my King
Uttering words of worship

My heart soars, my soul sings...

Being in His presence
He is speaking life to me
Everything about me He is validating
Replenishing every
Bump
Bruise
Scar
On my spiritual being...

He has replaced my old armor
He has given me a new one
He has traded my sorrows for His joy
He's given me His strength til my work here is done!

He has anointed my Prayer Shawl
He gave me double for my trouble
He charged me to speak on His behalf

To
no longer live in this world's bubble...

As I return my prayer shawl
To its secluded, secret place
Flashbacks of God's visitation
Resurfaced before my face...

And He blessed my soul
With ever word that proceeded from His mouth
Speaking to my soul
In Him, I have no doubt...

Breathe (A Word from God)

You've been bearing a weight
Constantly struggling with your faith
Withholding everything, not releasing
 Mind messing, love is decreasing
Your marriage is a mess
Thinking you've failed every test
Questioning what's in your spirit
'Cause people want to keep you in "it"
But daughter, I've called you
Not one loves you like I do
Their love was conditional
My love for you has and will always be eternal
You loved someone deeply
Their love wasn't of that, not remotely
Giving of yourself only to be used
Which made you see something which I didn't view you...

You are royalty

You are beauty

 You are quality

You are equality

You are my child You are the apple of my eye
 You are more and then some
You are Me but in female form
You are not crazy

You hear from Me daily
 Don't doubt when you hear
My voice
Because you know you have made the right choice
You've been abused

Mishandled

Mistreated Misused

But I have come to wipe your tears
 I have come to erase your fears
You have repented to me and you are now good
No one can condemn you, remember, I was stretched out on
wood

For you...

You haven't been able to breathe
Because he lied and had you deceived
Walking on eggshells so he don't trip
 But I'm releasing you from his grip
For all these years I've seen your tears
 They have ripped through my heart like stripped gears
You have proven your strength in this bitter time
 I have heard your cries and you are completely mine!
No one will get to you like they did in your past
Because you now know your strength, they will not last,
For you were fighting them all by yourself
 Now I'm fighting for you, no need to stress them
Breathe now, daughter
He can't smother you anymore
Cry loud, My child
Your tears are alarm to be heard
Your strength is commendable
The weight you carried was very unbearable
 But you called out to Me and I saved you
Now, bright and clear, I speak, you do...
You cried, I heard you You were dying,
I revived you You were breathless
I put my breath into you
Now you can breathe

So I can speak through you....

The Cure for Spiritual Cancer

Open Vision: God showed me to see a healthy cell within the human body. Vibrate, normal blood flow being administered to it and coming in connection with the other cells to stay healthy and vibrant. Then, He allowed me to see this same cell, but, there was a smaller cell, an unhealthy, black and diseased cell trying to invade the larger, healthy cell. It penetrated the healthy cell's membrane, travels to the nucleus of the healthy and plants itself within the healthy cell and then multiplies, causing the healthy cell to rapidly turn black, killing the healthy cell.

I know I have stated before that Satan has strategically planted demons and evil spirits in the house of God to infiltrate God's house and make the church an **UNWORKABLE** organism in the community!

In this latest illustration the Lord has shown me, this is the strategy Satan has come up with, thinking this will surely kill everyone who is seeking God and striving to please Him! What Satan doesn't realize is that we all are up to speed on what the outcome really is! We know that Jesus has the keys to hell and death *(Rev 1:18)*

Satan has come, in this season, to mess with our minds! To steal the very things that The Lord has given us to use for His glory!! The enemy has placed is demons to be distractions to the body so he can get us off track! But THE DEVIL IS A LIAR!!! He can set us off track, but, we have a way to get back on track and get back in line and not just in line, but back on the front line!!! Jesus is and always will be the answer!!!

Jesus is the cure for the cancerous cells that are trying to kill us off! Reading His word is the chemotherapy, His Holy Spirit is the Radiation! **THIS IS THE TREATMENT FOR THE SPIRITUAL CANCER THAT IS TRYING TO INVADE THE BODY OF CHRIST!!!**

 The thief cometh not, but for to steal, and to kill, and to destroy: I am come that they might have life, and that they might have it more abundantly.

Now!!! God has given us the information we need to battle in this war! **IT IS TIME TO SHOUT OUT OUR WAR CRY AND CONQUER ALL THINGS IN THE NAME OF JESUS!!!** Satan and his little demons have come to through us off but **OUR GOD IS BIGGER AND BADDER THAN ANYTHING SATAN HAS!!! FIGHT THE GOOD FIGHT!!** If anyone is battling cancer in your body, **SPEAK LIFE AND CAST IT TO THE VERY PITS OF HELL** in the name of Jesus! If anyone is dealing with spiritual sickness, **REBUKE THE DEVOURER IN THE NAME OF JESUS AND BE MADE WHOLE!! BELIEVE THAT GOD CAN AND WILL HEAL YOU IN THE NAME OF JESUS!! BELIEVE THAT GOD WILL FIGHT YOUR BATTLES FOR YOU IN THE NAME OF JESUS!! BELIEVE IN HIS WORD AND SPEAK HIS WORD IN EVERY SITUATION!! BE STEADFAST, UNMOVABLE** *(1Cor 15:58)*

Words of Encouragement

HUMBLE YOURSELF!!

Let nothing be done through selfish ambition or conceit, but in lowliness of mind let each esteem others better than himself. (Philippians 2:3 NKJV)

Humble: *having or showing a modest or low estimate of one's own importance.*

We have lost our sense of humility!! We have lost our sense of lowliness to the point where every conversation we have if focused on all the things we have done, the things we've said and the things people have said to or done for us to exalt us!

In light, we must be very careful when we exalt ourselves or when we make ourselves more than what we really are because we take God out of the equation! God SHOULD BE FIRST in our lives, not man and certainly not ourselves! God is the rewarder of those who diligently seek HIM not man *(Heb.11:6)!*

I was in Sunday school and the teacher said something that continues to stick with me. He gave this example: Suppose you're driving and you see someone you're not particularly cool with stranded on the side of the road with a flat tire. You decide to help that person out because you don't like the person, but, you don't wish any harm on that person either. You act because of the love of Christ, but, you don't have to go telling everybody what you did. When you do that, you received your reward; you got your pat on the back! Whereas if you just did what you did and went on your merry way, God would recognize what you did and HE WOULD HAVE REWARDED YOU! HUMILITY!!! We are not to say and do things to get accolades from man!! We are to do things because of the love of Christ in us and because we are to think of others just a little higher than ourselves!

Humble yourselves in the sight of the Lord, and He will lift you up. *(James 4:10 NKJV)*

Why exalt ourselves? There's only so much we can do or say to make ourselves seem spectacular... But, if we are humble and remain humble unto God, HE WILL LIFT YOU UP! He will exalt you! He will set you up and you won't have to say a thing!!!

When Jesus gave His life for us, He didn't do it so that His Father would congratulate Him and pat Him on the back, like a father would his son after witnessing him making the winning touchdown in a football game... Jesus gave His life for us because of the love He has for us and the humility He had! He is the Son of Man, but His Father had a plan for His life, that He would give His life to save ours. Now, if that's not a prime example of humility, I don't know what is....

Renew Your Vows!!

As I was sitting here thinking about the last two Sundays and how God has moved in such a peculiar way, I heard Him whisper in my ear "Renew Your Vow".

After hearing that in my spirit, I began to think on yesterday's service at 10:30 where the hearts of the worshippers were in obedience to the Lord and His spirit! I recall hearing someone in pure worship wailing "Yes!" Over and over again. Then He took me back to last Sunday where myself and my tag team partner preached about just say yes to God, where we ought to give our bodies and living sacrifices and not being conformed to this world but being transformed by the renewing of the mind.

We are in a place and time where your yes has to be yes and your no has to be no. There is no more straddling the fence, there's no more being lukewarm, we must be hot or cold. Either we believe in God or we don't...

The Lord is speaking and He is saying **_NOW IS THE TIME TO RENEW YOUR VOW TO HIM!!_** God is a jealous God and He will not come second to **ANYONE** or **ANYTHING!!** He desires a yes from you but it can't just be a yes with your mouth, but, your yes has to be with YOUR EVERYTHING!! Your heart, your mind, your spirit and your soul!!

Allow yourself to hear from the Lord and hear what He has to say to you concerning your life. The devil is trying to kill you but he can't touch you unless you allow him to! When Satan tried to tempt Jesus after He fasted for 40 days and 40 nights, had Jesus fell for the Okie Doke, thus allowing Satan to rule over Him, Satan would have had the victory! But because Jesus knew this and would rather fulfill the call of God, He rebuked Satan and told him to get behind Him! It's time to tell Satan to get behind you because he is in your ear telling you you're worthless, you don't have what it takes, your tears don't mean anything, your cries out don't mean nothing and it don't take all of that!! **THE**

DEVIL IS A LIAR!! Don't you know when you shout, when you cry out, when you open your mouth God hears you!! Your sound activates change!!! **OPEN YOUR MOUTH AND MAKE YOUR SOUND UNTO GOD!! RENEW YOUR VOWS AND SAY YES TO GOD AGAIN AND MEAN IT BECAUSE HE WILL BE MOVED TO INTERVENE IN YOUR SITUATION!!!** God is the ONLY ONE who can make it happen for you!

Renew your vow to the Lord and He will honor it! Seek Him with everything you got!! He will move on your behalf in any situation or circumstance!! He will heal your broken heart! He will place you at the right place at the right time! He will give you favor and bless you endlessly! He already been doing that because He's allowed you to breathe, He's allowed you to move and He's allowed you to think even in the midst of your garbage, in the midst of your indecisiveness!!

Man will mess up, man will fail you, man will say one thing and do something else but God never fails! God never says something and takes it back for He is not a man that He should lie! He's not going to call you to do for Him and not see you through!

Renew your vow to God and say yes!!

He Has You on His Mind

For I know the thoughts that I think toward you, saith the LORD, thoughts of peace, and not of evil, to give you an expected end (Jeremiah 29:11 KJV)

We live in a world where what we say and what we do is sometimes predicated on what others think of us or say about us. Because our actions are based on others thoughts and opinions of us, we tend to become unhappy and unsatisfied with ourselves.

We don't take it into consideration, at times, that man does not and cannot determine your worth or your ability to do what you have been blessed and called to do. People tend to make you feel inferior because you didn't do or say what they thought you should have. So what do they do? They will either talk down to you or they will tell you what you should have said or should have done, thus, making you think like you aren't capable of handling your situations or making you think you're not wise in handling matters concerning you. We are human! We are fallible! WE ARE NOT PERFECT!

But, unfortunately, there are folks in this world that feel they know more about you than you do. There are people in this world that swear they know what's best for you but have yet to walk a day in your shoes. People who normally think they can just tell you what to do, what to say, thus ultimately, tell you who to be think little of you. As a matter of fact, they don't think much of you at all! These people are who you would call Spiritual Bullies! Their thoughts of you tear the very fabric of who you are.... If you're not careful!

In this verse, God says He knows the PLANS HE HAS FOR YOU!! Not man, but God has plans for you! You have a purpose that He designed and shaped just for you! Not only that, but, He has equipped you with the ability to fulfill the plans He has for you! God doesn't make any junk, so, since He has called you to do such wonderful things, FOR HIM, you must not allow simple man to undermine or demean you in any way!! The thoughts He has for you are thoughts of PEACE and NOT EVIL!! What man seems to forget is when they become Spiritual Bullies; they disrupt the peace that is within you. What? Did you think someone would still be able to have peace within when there is someone who constantly makes you feel like you can't do anything right because they spend all their time correcting you and telling you what to do? There is no peace in that! For God's thoughts for you are of peace and not evil, so just know, if someone is saying or doing something to make you feel like you are beneath them and it makes your spirit uneasy, know that it's not of God! I say that because if your spirit is uneasy, the possibility of your mind being affected by this is almost inevitable. This brings for confusion within and we know God is not the author of confusion!

Now, if God's thoughts for you are of peace and not evil, what do you believe is the end result for you, according to Him? To give you and EXPECTED END!! Your expected end is the finality of your God given assignment in life. God's thoughts for you are that of the very ability to complete the task He has called you to do, for the up building of His Kingdom and for you to continue to do the task to the best of your ability until your last day! He expects you to do well! He expects you to succeed! He expects you to know your potential and He expects you to know that just from the very thoughts He has of you!!! His thoughts for you are to SUCCEED!! His thoughts for you are to SURVIVE!! His thoughts for you are to THRIVE!!! He doesn't wish any ill will on you! He gives you the instructions to do what you are called to do with love and compassion, not with intimidation and fear! It's time for us all to think on the things of God! Think of how He views you. Think of how He loves you. Think of the way He has provision for you. God loves you so much that His thoughts are of peace and not evil! And the verse doesn't say how long He will have these thoughts for you, so, to me, His thoughts for you are INDEFINITE!!

I'm sure there have been or there are people in your life who like to flex their supposedly mental or intellectual muscles by bullying you into taking what they think or how they feel because they just don't know any better. I dare you to think of this verse and take on a totally different mindset from now on!!

Take a stand against the Spiritual Bully and enforce your God given ability to maneuver in peace simply because of how He thinks of you.

Your Testing Season is At Hand

You have always put a wall of protection around him and his home and his property. You have made him prosper in everything he does. Look how rich he is! (Job 1:10 NLT)

"All right, you may test him," the Lord said to Satan. "Do whatever you want with everything he possesses, but don't harm him physically." So Satan left the Lord's presence. (Job 1:12 NLT)

One of my favorite movies to watch is Independence Day. I, normally, don't frequent "sci fi" type movies but this one, to me, was good.

There is a scene in this movie where the cable repairman, who ironically, was a graduate from MIT, found a way to get rid of the aliens and their spacecrafts by flying into space, giving their systems a computer virus, set of some kind of an explosion and then destroy them before they destroyed Earth.

See, his plan to do all of that was to simply disable their protective shields that were upon every spacecraft. Before that, American soldiers were dropping like flies from retaliation because they were shooting at the aliens.

Once their defenses were down, our soldiers were able to fire their weapons and shoot down the alien spaceships.

To have the intelligence to come up with an idea like that, as crazy as it sounded, is a bit beyond genius! But, could you imagine this in our Christian walk? Would you be able to operate and function without the "protective shield" of Our Father? Would you consider that being the "Genius Idea" that God would have for your life? To take His protection away from you to see how you conduct yourself under pressure, to see if you would "curse Him and die"?

Well, first and foremost, all things God does is GENIUS and there is always a method to the madness we go through in our day to day lives!

Now, we all know the story of Job. He was blameless in the sight of God! He honored God, he was well respected amongst his peers but most of all, he feared God! Satan and God had a little conversation (Job 1: 6 -12 NLT). In vs. 7 God asks Satan where has he been, what has he been up to? Satan told God that he had been patrolling the earth, seeking whom he may devour... Can you even fathom that?

Someone that is purposely searching to trip people up...

Someone that is constantly wanting, needing to cause havoc in someone's life ON PURPOSE and WITHOUT APOLOGY?

Well, could you really believe that God gave Satan permission to go after Job? If not, check your bible... vs. 12 clearly shows God giving Satan permission to TEST Job... BUT! God set perimeters or conditions to this test... Satan was not to touch Job physically, but, everything else was open season...

Everyone will have a Job experience; some will experience this more than once. Every season we enter into, there will be another test, more intense than the former. Reason being is so God will know how much He can trust you with what He gives you, He will be able to see how you conduct yourself in the struggle but most of all to see if you will rely on Him, call on Him, praise Him, glorify Him, worship Him and NOT CURSE HIM!

I'm a DIY type person (do it yourself) and I love watching certain YouTube videos to learn how to make natural products for my hair and skin. Last night, I watched the process for making Castor Oil, COLD PRESSED! TALK ABOUT INTRIGUING!! The process looked simple, but, it's very pressing and hard. The castor seeds or beans are roasted first, then, they are placed in a sturdy bow or tub and they are mashed, almost like a pestle and mortar set up. This is the most tedious part because every bean has to be crushed before doing the next step and it takes a lot of muscle to do this! Once the beans have been mashed completely, you transfer the mash into a pot of water and boil the mash until the water boils out, stirring occasionally so there is no sticking at the bottom of the pot. Then you take a bowl, a fine mesh or cheesecloth, put some of the mash in it and squeeze all of the oil out of the mash.

So!!

Using this as an example of how we are processes in our lives, when we choose to live for the Lord, is like the process of this Castor Bean. We are put in heat, we are pressed, we get into deep, hot water and then we are squeezed until we are empty. We go through this type of process to remove any and all impurities so when the finished product comes out, we will be so much more effective to be used by God!

In this crushing, this pressing, this testing season, we will be in a great place to be humbled! This is the season where those who are not in Christ will be picking and prodding us and trying to find ways to expose he people of God! **I say people who aren't in Christ because those who say they are in Christ but are doing these same vicious things are not operating in the Holy Ghost, therefore making them shepherds for the devil! Witches and warlocks are amongst us and if we are not careful, we will be consumed by them!** if we have the heart of God and we are called to bring in those who are lost, it would behoove us to get our act together! God is putting us through this testing season to gear us up for the levels we will go to next FOR THE KINGDOM! In order to do that, WE MUST BE HUMBLE! This is not about us, not even a little bit!!

In this season, during your test, keep your eyes on God! Keep your ears to His voice, and when you can't hear Him, continue to talk to Him, because Even though you can't hear Him, He still hears you! Keep your hands to the plow and use them to uplift His Kingdom! Keep your feet planted on His word because His word is a lamp unto you feet and a light unto your path! Finally, lift your voice to Him and curse Him not! Bless His name in everything you go through, good or bad! Job said it best, *"Though He slay me, yet will I trust Him..."* (Job 13:15)

We must have that same stance, especially if we say we trust and believe Him...

Prove it!! Don't faint!! Don't quit!! Don't Curse Him!!

Training for Battle

They said, 'Whenever we are faced with any calamity such as war, plague, or famine, we can come to stand in your presence before this Temple where your name is honored. We can cry out to you to save us, and you will hear us and rescue us.' (2 Chronicles 20:9 NLT)

On the day of Pentecost all the believers were meeting together in one place (Acts 2:1 NLT)

For the last two Sundays, I have been seeing and reading on social media about the services of those I follow, including the church I belong to and for these particular Sundays, at different churches, some in different states, we all have had the same God experience!

Last Sunday, my pastor couldn't even preach as the presence of the Lord was so thick in the place! The atmosphere was conducive for miracles, healing and deliverance, which, I believe in my heart of hearts, took place! Then on yesterday there was a breaking like no other!!! Ironic I would say there was a breaking that took place, when the sermon on yesterday was "It's Not Going to Break Me!" taken from 2 Corinthians 12:7-10....

As our pastor was just beginning preaching, the spirit of the Lord dropped this nugget in my Spirit, " Your leader will have more Sundays like this and the previous Sunday, where he will barely preach, for I am training you in Spiritual Warfare hands on!!" We have to admit that everyone who comes to church isn't coming for the reasons they should, because of this, there will always be a "spectator spirit" looming in our churches when there is a visitation of God through the Holy Spirit. But for those who know the power of God and have ever experienced His presence knows that when He is in the building YOU MUST TAP INTO IT!

First of all, you must come with the Spirit of Expectation...

Let all that I am wait quietly before God,
for my hope is in him (Psalm 62:5 NLT)

Our hearts have to be so open to receiving God and all that He is so we could be able to receive the blessings, miracles and healing we desire from Him! Along with this we must have the right premise... the attitude, the reasoning for our expectation of God! We anticipate the presence of God not only because He is our Father and we know He has the power and the will to make all things happen for us, but, we know that in lieu of our expectation, our response to receiving the blessings of God is that of acknowledgement and servitude!

We don't expect because we deserve it! For we know that it's because of His grace and mercy we are even able to go to him, through Christ Jesus, but, we expect because He bids is to come to Him so He can give us rest from the very things that plague us...

Then Jesus said, "Come to me, all of you who are weary and carry heavy burdens, and I will give you rest. (Matthew 11:28 NLT)

But even with Him bidding is to come to Him, there is still a condition we all must meet when we do partake of His power and His strength...

Take my yoke upon you. Let me teach you, because I am humble and gentle at heart, and you will find rest for your souls (Matthew 11:29 NLT)

Expecting, receiving and serving equips us to stand in the presence of God.

The Spirit of the Lord is very clear in this hour!

We are in the fight of our lives, but, it's not a physical one! This war is not one we battle with M-16's or grenades. This war is one we must battle in the Spirit Realm! We must be tactful with our weapons and know their purpose and know how to use them! The Spirit of the Lord is saying in this hour the weapons He is training you in He will be training you in the midst of the battle! While you are in prayer in your private time, alone, while you are in a group of two or three and especially while you are in an environment, a church setting, full of believers! He is training you in your worship, in your praise, He is extending your Heavenly language, He is stretching you to be more reliable on His power so when the enemy attacks, you will be able to take him down once and for all EFFECTIVELY!!

Open vision:

As I'm typing this to you, I saw, in the Spirit, a battleground. The ground is bald, dry, no sign of anything with life springing forth from it, totally desolate! There are Angels on one side, demons on the other. As worship is going on in the Earthly Realm, the Angels are bombarding the demons. When tongues are being spoken, the demons are falling to the ground and there is a blood curdling squeal coming from the demons as they hit the ground!

THIS IS WHERE WE ARE NOW!! Your attack starts with the word of God, reading your bible every moment you get! Fasting and praying is part of your preparation, because demons know whether or not you are truly one of God's children and they will taunt you (Acts 19:14 -17). We must be sharp on our ability to wage in war at any given time the enemy rears his pointy little head because if we don't sharpen our tools, the enemy will defeat us and we can't let that happen!

King Jehoshaphat was told that neighboring kingdoms were joining together to attack his kingdom. The first thing he did was issue the order for everyone in Judah to fast! Then, he went into prayer. He reminded God if things He said concerning his ancestors, even about the promise His made with His friend Abraham. He reminded God that every time they faced a battle, a crisis or some type of issue, that they have always looked to Him, gotten in His presence because they know who their Deliverer was!!! (2 Chronicles 20:9 NLT)

We must know this and keep it in the forefront of our minds and hearts! God honors our worship, when it's sincere, He will fight our battles and defend us, but, we must serve Him, learn of Him, keep His commandments, REPENT when we fall and acknowledge Him in all things!!!!

These past two Sundays, there was a thirst, a desire for God's presence that seemed to be unquenchable! There was a need, not for things or objects, but, there was a need of visitation, of ministering to that deep place in our hearts and souls that no human could ever touch!!

As the deer longs for streams of water,
so I long for you, O God
I thirst for God, the living God.
When can I go and stand before him?
(Psalm 42:1,2 NLT)

Who doesn't want to serve a God like that? Who can quench your thirst in a dry and weary land? I love how it says in vs. 2 "I thirst for God, the living God"!!!

MY GOD IS NOT DEAD!!!

Get into His presence! Not only will you see the fullness of joy, that's one reason to get in His face, but, getting in God's face will acknowledge to Him that you have put all of your will, all of your trust and all of your faith in Him to fight your battles and to defeat the enemy!!!

IT'S TIME FOR WAR!!!

The Spirit of Offense

My heart is heavy and my spirit is grieved... HOW ARE WE COMPELLING PEOPLE TO COME TO CHRIST WHEN WE ARE WALKING IN THE SPIRIT OF OFFENSE ALL THE TIME??

So what people don't always agree with you! So what people may not understand you, the anointing or the call on your life! IT'S NOT FOR THEM TO UNDERSTAND BUT IT'S FOR GOD TO GET THE GLORY OUT OF IT!!

Offense is a cancer in the church and it is a blocker of blessings and forward movement in the body of Christ! We cannot go out and draw men and women to Christ if we can't get it together!!

So be careful how you live. Don't live like fools, but like those who are wise. Make the most of every opportunity in these evil days. Don't act thoughtlessly, but understand what the Lord wants you to do (Ephesians 5:15 - 5:17 NLT)

Offense manifests itself in different ways, control, manipulation, quarrelsome/argumentative, judgmental, self-entitlement and self-righteousness. Offense will have you checking everyone else out so you won't have to deal with yourself! Offense will have to speaking to everybody in a way that makes you look like a boss, but, you come across as a bully. Offense is NOT OF GOD!! Jesus didn't walk in offense when He was betrayed by Judas, he knew why it had to take place, but, Jesus is the Son of God and He knew that He had to walk in that manner... Why?? Because He was God in the flesh and God commanded us to love one another, He commanded we worship Him in spirit and in truth and that we walk in the Spirit of God, NOT OF FLESH!!

Lastly, offense is a fleshly thang!!

Those who walk in the spirit of offense do so because there has been no crucifixion of the flesh!!

And I will give you a new heart, and I will put a new spirit in you. I will take out your stony, stubborn heart and give you a tender, responsive heart. And I will put my Spirit in you so that you will follow my decrees and be careful to obey my regulations. (Ezekiel 36:26-27 NLT)

Let's get this thing straight... if you claim to have Christ in your heart, if you claim to have the Holy Spirit, then your focus should be on the things of Christ, the will of Christ and the spirit of Christ, NOT YOURSELF! If you're walking in the Spirit of Christ, then there would be no room for offense because you would be in prayer, you would be fasting, you would be studying His word and digesting it so you will not be offended, thus, being effective in the ministry of reconciliation, bringing unbelievers to Christ and building the kingdom of God!!

Let's check ourselves THOROUGHLY and be about our Father's business

It's Time for Battle!!!

Revelation

We are in a time where the manifestation of Heaven and Hell are at war is coming to pass!

Just like the prophets of the Lord are emerging, witches and warlocks are rearing their ugly little heads, coming out of the woodwork to cause chaos in the house of God. They are masking themselves as men and women of God, pretending to be about God's business and the up building of the kingdom.

They are at the right place, at the right time, to assist the man and woman of God in their ministries. They are trying to earn their trust, making themselves available at any given moment to them so they will release the secrets the Lord has released to them for building up the kingdom of God. These witches and warlocks are trying to move through the ranks **WITHOUT GOING THROUGH THE PROCESS OF THE LORD,** *WHICH WOULD SHOW THEM TO BE TRUE SOLDIERS FOR THE LORD!!*

The traits and characteristics these men and women will exhibit are as such...

· *Pride*

· *Haughtiness*

· *Rebellion*

· *Offense (the spirit of)*

· *Deceptiveness*

· *Manipulation*

· *Contempt*

The sad thing about all of this is they don't even realize they are acting unseemly. They will show some or all of these characteristics when they are subjected to correction, rebuke, and lack of being used in the capacity in which they feel they should be used in. They will feel like once they have been called and affirmed of said calling, they should immediately walk in that calling and train as they go, forgoing any type of training from their covering, thus, becoming a rouge, or a bastard in the spirit.

The revelation the Holy Spirit gave me concerning this

In **Revelations 12:7-12**, John talks about how Michael and God's angels were at war with "the dragon" or Satan and his angels. God's angels defeated Satan and his angels and were kicked out of Heaven down to Earth.

Now, we know, Satan doesn't have any power until he is able to use someone to do his dirty work, he sends his demons to possess those who are open in their spirit, who want to fulfill their fleshly desires. This allows the vessel to be used by Satan to do what he wants to do. Because of this the people of God really need to be on point!!!

We must continue to seek God's face! We must continue to pray without ceasing! We must fast! We must continue to be purged vessels of God, not just spiritually, but naturally as well! We must purge out those things that are not like God and fill that space with His word, with His

Spirit and with His heart! We must continue to hunger and thirst for HIM!

Psalms 24:1 says

As the deer longs for streams of water, so I long for you, O God. 2 I thirst for God, the living God. When can I go and stand before him?

This must be our posture! In order for us not to be in the position of being categorized as a witch, warlock, demon or anything that does not describe us as children of God, we must fashion ourselves to seek after God like never before!!

Now, don't get me wrong, David tells us in Psalms 24:1 that the Earth is the Lord's and the fullness thereof. But, we were introduced to sin back in the Garden of Eden, thus subjecting us to sin nature.

Ezekiel 28:15 says

Thou wast perfect in thy ways from the day that thou was created, til iniquity was found in thee.

With the fact that Satan was kicked out of Heaven and he is running to and fro seeking whom he can devour, we must be on guard for our very souls!

Listen...

The word of the Lord is to watch and pray! There will be a shift in the house of God, but, those who are not real with Him or with themselves will miss it!! People of God, unless He tells you to release the plans He has for His people and for the building up of His kingdom, do not say a word!!! Satan is waiting to hear what's going on and he has placed his demons in position to befriend the man and the woman of God to hear the instructions from the Lord and to dismantle the very plans that God has spoken to His servants.

LOOSE LIPS SINK SHIPS!!!

Be watchful of those you have in leadership position! Watch for the characteristics that were mentioned in the beginning of this word so you will know who, what, when, where, why and how!!!

THIS IS RED ALERT TO THE HOUSE OF GOD!!!

PROPHETS OF THE MOST HIGH GOD!!! IT'S TIME TO COME OUT AND SPEAK WHAT THUS SAYS THE LORD!!! THIS IS THE TIME YOU MUST STAND UP AND SPEAK AGAINST THE VERY THING THAT WILL CAUSE THE HOUSE OF GOD TO CRUMBLE! CALL OUT THOSE DEMONS, CALL THEM OUT BY NAME! CUT JEZEBEL'S HEAD OFF WITH THE VERY WORD OF THE LORD!!! CANCEL THE SPIRIT OF AHAB, WHO IS BEING THE BIG BABY AND SPOILED BRAT HE IS BECAUSE HE CAN'T HAVE WHAT HE WANTS, WHEN HE WANTS!!! THE LORD IS SOVEREIGN! HE IS THE ONLY ONE THAT CAN DO WHAT HE WANTS, WHEN HE WANTS AND HOW HE WANTS!

It is time take authority over the very things God has given to us to take dominion over!!! If you can't take authority, you are not in possession of the Holy Ghost and you must GET IN POSITION TO FULLY ACCEPT THE WILL OF GOD AND ACCEPT HIS SWEET HOLY GHOST!!!

We have already seen the work of God's angels and His armies when they won the war in Heaven and kicked Satan out of Heaven! We have that same ability to defeat the enemy because of the power of the Holy Ghost!

This has to happen because these witches, warlocks, imps and demons are coming for the people of God with a vengeance!

But, Paul tells us this in *Ephesians 6:12, 13*:

For we wrestle not against flesh and blood, but against principalities, against powers, against the rulers of the darkness of this world, against spiritual wickedness in high places. Wherefore take unto you the whole armour of God that ye may be able to withstand in the evil day, and having done all, to stand.

It's time to go to battle!!!!

To God be the Glory for the works He will perform through us in this battle because this will show the power of God in all of His splendor!!!!

Don't Give Up!!!

Wow!!!! The revelation of the word of the Lord is AWESOME!!! I was reading 2 Kings 20 where it speaks about King Hezekiah. I read on past Isaiah telling him God was adding 15 more years to his life and I saw something I never read before!!! The Lord tell Isaiah to give hezekiah instructions to what to do to fully recover from his illness... First, he told him that in 3 days he will be healed and to get out of bed and go to the Temple. Then he said that He will add 15 yrs to his life and save the city.

THEN!!! In vs. 7 he says this

Then Isaiah said, "Make an ointment from figs." So Hezekiah's servants spread the ointment over the boil, and Hezekiah recovered! (2 Kings 20:7 NLT)

WHAT????

So, Isaiah told Hezekiah to get his house in order because the Lord said he was gonna die and God had a cure for him to recover THE WHOLE TIME!!! This gives new meaning to this scripture for me!! I've always known this to be a scripture on faith in God but MAN!!! Could you imagine if Hezekiah didn't go to God in prayer and remind God of his servitude to Him?? Hezekiah would not have been alive and wouldn't have been blessed to receive the instruction from the prophet to become healed!

HE DIDN'T GIVE UP!!! His trust in God didn't waiver!!

If the king didn't give up, why should we?? Prayer is so important especially when there are things we don't tend to understand while enduring the trials and tribulations in our Christian walk. If Hezekiah was not a man of God and didn't know the power of prayer, the lack of that fact would have led to his demise. Knowing God for yourself is so imperative! But, there's a clause attached to that... After he prayed, HE LISTENED!!! He listened to the instructions the prophet of the Lord gave him, not only to solidify his recovery but to continue his relationship with God! The first part of the instructions was for him to go to the temple in 3 days after he was able to get out of bed... going to the temple after sickness in that time was necessary to be cleansed and to be declared ceremonially clean. Being declared clean gives him the right to be amongst people without them yelling UNCLEAN whenever he was sighted! This was also a means to declare to the people that God is a healer and He does acknowledge the works of those who believe in Him. He turned it around for Hezekiah BY HIS SPOKEN WORD!!

Then after he went to the temple, Hezekiah listened further and heard the instructions to make an ointment that his servant rubbed on him and that sealed the deal of God's promise to him!

Not only was he healed but he was given 15 additional years to his life!!!

What kind of person would not want to serve a God like this????

The Shofar of Poetry

God Inspired Poems & Words of Encouragement to Break the Chains of Bondage

A Word from the Lord for His Elect:

There is a heavy burden on God's elect! We are the very *PREY* of those who say we are not called of God! We are the ones being attacked when our accusers "*PRAY*" not for us but against us because they feel more righteous to do so! Not understanding the more they *PREY* on us, the more we *PRAY* for them! They have no idea that they are giving us *POWER*! The more they *PREY* on us, the more they make room for us to be elevated!!! The more they *PREY* on us, the more they allow God to create the *OPEN PLACES* for *PUBLIC BLESSINGS!!!*

They need to *PREY* on God's called because they feel they are better equipped to handle the task God has called you to do. That makes them *GUILTY OF THE BLOOD OF JESUS!*

TO THE ACCUSER OF THE BRETHREN: You have broken His Holy Commandment when He said *THOU SHALT NOT COVET*... *PREYING* on someone because of the *ANOINTING* on their life means to destroy the very vision God placed in you because you chose to attack their vision by slandering their name and putting your mouth on God's anointed!! *REPENT!! TURN FROM YOUR WICKED WAYS AND GET RIGHY WITH GOD!!* Stop *PREYING* on others and worry about *WHAT GOD IS SAYING TO YOU*!!! Worry about what God is telling you to do!

A Note from the Writer...

God bless you richly for taking the time to read these writings, I believe, the Spirit of the Lord has blessed me to write.

I believe in my heart and soul the words on these pages are straight from the mouth of the Lord. Him revealing these insightful messages and poems to me were not just for me, for my Spirit, He has released me to chare these very writings with you.

It is very humbling to be in a position not only to hear from God, whether it be through, prayer, dreams or even an open vision, but it's humbling to be able to express gratitude to Him by releasing His words to His people.

There are no words that could ever describe the exuberance in my heart about this particular release of this book. I am sure this book will speak to your very Spirit and enlighten your soul to the place where you will be open to search within yourself to go deeper in your Spirit to hear from the Lord.

In His Service,

Tammy (T.T.Taylor)

Why Did I Call This Book The Shofar of Poetry?

In the Bible, the shofar has been used to announce certain occurrences, for instance, one long singe blast was sounded for the King's coronation (Tekiah), three short wail-like blasts signified repentance (Shevarim), nine staccato blasts of alarm was to awaken the soul (Teru'ah) and a great long blast for as long as you can blow (Tekiah ha-Gadol).

There are many instances in the Bible where it tells you the trumpet (Shofar) was blown, always in spiritual warfare.

[9] *And if ye go to war in your land against the enemy that oppresseth you, then ye shall blow an alarm with the trumpets; and ye shall be remembered before the LORD your God and ye shall be saved from your enemies.*
(Numbers 10:9 KJV)

While writing this book, I was in the process of fasting and praying and asking God to give me a title for this book. I was watching television one night, when I couldn't sleep and I heard the word "Shofar" in my Spirit. I have seen this word before and I knew what it was but I didn't know the very significance of the shofar... As I began to dig a little deeper into studying more about it, I ran into a clip on a social media outlet. There was a woman of God explaining what a shofar is and the process it goes through for it to be made for the purpose in which it is intended for... SPIRITUAL WARFARE! Then it came to me quickly after watching that particular clip... 'The Shofar of Poetry... God Inspired Poems & Words of Encouragement to Break the Chains of Bondage".

But, I was a little perplexed... I didn't understand why the Holy Spirit would have me title the book this way? It wasn't until I began to edit the book and really read through the entries again when I realized the poem selections I chose were my testimonies of overcoming defeat, climbing out of darkness and accepting the call on my life, even if it may not be popular. The other entries in this book were words from the Lord to encourage me, now others, of the very walk we must take when we say yes to Christ.

But the Shofar part was still troubling to me...
Shofar?
Spiritual warfare?
How does this fit?

Blow ye the trumpet in Zion, and sound an alarm in my holy mountain: let all the inhabitants of the land tremble: for the day of the LORD cometh, for it is nigh at hand.
(Joel 2:1 KJV)

The Spirit of God revealed to me these writings are directly from Him, thus, sounding the alarm on His truth! These writings are a form of Spiritual Warfare because these are the writings He gave me to overcome my spiritual battles. The poems were to get out the oppression I had felt for years, later revealing the hand of God pulling me out of that oppression.

It made perfect sense to me.

In conclusion, I pray you are blessed in reading the word of from the Lord and that you will begin and continue to grow in Him!

About the Author

Minister Tamara Taylor, an associate minister at Mount Olive Church Ministries, under the Rev. Dion J. Watkins, is a lifelong resident of Hartford, CT. A devoted wife, mother of two, grew up in the historical neighborhood of Charter Oak Terrace. A product of the Hartford Public School System and graduating from Bulkeley High School in 1993, she went straight into the workforce, when she decided to serve her country for a short time in the United States Army where she was stationed in FT. Jackson, South Carolina.

In 2004, she was called, by God, to preach the gospel of Jesus Christ. In 2005, she preached her initial sermon and became a licensed minister under Pastor Autherine Lattimore, of From the Heart Ministries in Hartford CT. Shortly after which, she would go through a spiritual attack unlike no other! She left the church and began to live a lifestyle that would and could have killed her.

BUT GOD!!

IN 2014, the Holy Spirit summoned her to come back to the Lord. She followed the instructions of the Lord, remembering the very verse the Lord gave her the very night she was called. Jeremiah 1:5 "Before I formed thee in the belly I knew thee; and before thou camest forth out of the womb I sanctified thee, and I ordained thee a prophet unto the nations."

Her love of writing came by way of her love for singing and music. She has been singing since childhood, but since she was so shy, she channeled her passion for rhythmic expression into writing.

She decided to share a few of her writings with close friends and received many positive responses. She has written over 200 poems and spoken word pieces.

Min. Taylor is currently the author of two self published books, From the Heart: Poetry from Within and True Thoughts of a Poet's Heart. This book is the first of many spiritual, prophetic, encouraging and God inspired books to come!

©T.T.Taylor

Contact Information

Email- **mailto:tttaylorauthor0603@gmail.com**

Facebook-*http://www.facebook.com/tamarat0603*

Twitter- *@triplet0603*

Instagram- *the_next_nikki_giovanni1*

Amazon Author Page - *https://www.amazon.com/Mrs-Tamara-T-Taylor/e/B076DFF1MD/ref=ntt_dp_epwbk_0*

The Shofar of Poetry

God Inspired Poems & Words of Encouragement to Break the Chains of Bondage

³⁸ Whoever believes in me, as the Scripture has said, 'Out of his heart will flow rivers of living water.' (John 7:38 NLT)

Made in the USA
Middletown, DE
24 March 2018